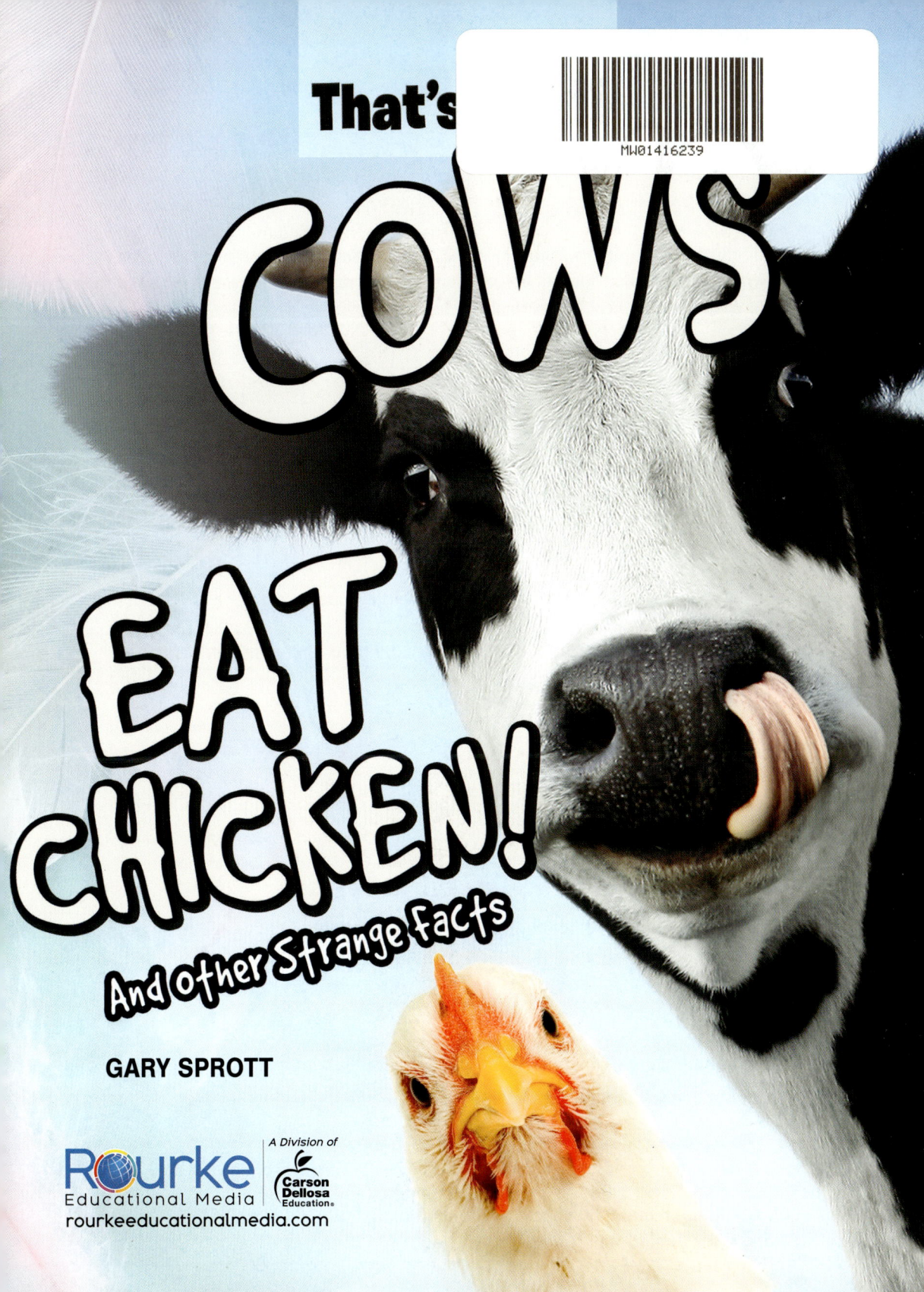

That's Cows Eat Chicken!

And other strange facts

GARY SPROTT

ROURKE'S SCHOOL to HOME CONNECTIONS
BEFORE AND DURING READING ACTIVITIES

Before Reading: *Building Background Knowledge and Vocabulary*

Building background knowledge can help children process new information and build upon what they already know. Before reading a book, it is important to tap into what children already know about the topic. This will help them develop their vocabulary and increase their reading comprehension.

Questions and Activities to Build Background Knowledge:

1. Look at the front cover of the book and read the title. What do you think this book will be about?
2. What do you already know about this topic?
3. Take a book walk and skim the pages. Look at the table of contents, photographs, captions, and bold words. Did these text features give you any information or predictions about what you will read in this book?

Vocabulary: *Vocabulary Is Key to Reading Comprehension*

Use the following directions to prompt a conversation about each word.

- Read the vocabulary words.
- What comes to mind when you see each word?
- What do you think each word means?

Vocabulary Words:
- bovines
- camouflage
- domestic
- mammals
- marsupial
- primates

During Reading: *Reading for Meaning and Understanding*

To achieve deep comprehension of a book, children are encouraged to use close reading strategies. During reading, it is important to have children stop and make connections. These connections result in deeper analysis and understanding of a book.

 ### Close Reading a Text

During reading, have children stop and talk about the following:

- Any confusing parts
- Any unknown words
- Text to text, text to self, text to world connections
- The main idea in each chapter or heading

Encourage children to use context clues to determine the meaning of any unknown words. These strategies will help children learn to analyze the text more thoroughly as they read.

When you are finished reading this book, turn to the next-to-last page for **After Reading Questions** and an **Activity**.

Table of Contents

Devils, Dragons, and Giants 4
Down on the Farm 14
Howlers, Poopers, and Sleepers 20
Memory Game 30
Index 31
After Reading Questions 31
Activity 31
About the Author 32

Devils, Dragons, and Giants

Lizards as long as a car! Kickboxing kangaroos! Meat-eating cows! And a chubby little critter that poops cubes! We share the land on our planet with some freaky, phenomenal animals.

Horned and Humongous

Standing up to six feet (two meters) tall and weighing as much as a pickup truck, it's no surprise that a rhinoceros has no natural predators. But just in case something starts nosing around its territory, the rhino can charge with its massive horn. This pointed snout can grow almost as long as the rhino is tall!

Armadillos are shy **mammals** with tough body armor and ingenious ways of defending against attack. The three-banded armadillo rolls itself into a tight ball to protect its belly and other soft body parts. The pink fairy armadillo scurries into its burrow. It then uses the flat plate of armor near its butt to cover the entrance like a door. Now that's a stinky welcome!

Armadillo means "little armored one."

mammals (MAM-uhls): warm-blooded animals that have fur or hair and usually give birth to live babies

With big, bouncy feet, kangaroos from Down Under can get up and over—quickly. These natives of Australia can hop as fast as a car, as high as a basketball net, and as far as a school bus is long! And when they're hopping mad, roos can deliver bone-crushing blows like a kickboxer!

Cute? Cuddly? Eh, No.

A Tasmanian devil is one mean **marsupial**! Named for an island off Australia's coast—and for its raging temper—this little demon has the most powerful bite for its size of any mammal. Tasmanian devils are so tough, they sometimes yawn at attackers!

marsupial (mahr-SOO-pee-uhl): one of a group of animals that includes the kangaroo, koala, and opossum; female marsupials carry their young in pouches on their abdomens

It's not a real-live dinosaur. It's a Komodo dragon, and this lizard can be a monstrous muncher. Pigs, deer, water buffalo, other dragons, and even humans might be on the menu. The dragon's razor-sharp claws and shark-like teeth are scary enough. But this heavyweight hunter also produces venom that sends its prey into shock!

A Rare But Deadly Bite

Many reptiles are venomous. But scientists believe there's only one living mammal that can inject a toxic substance with a bite. The solenodon looks like a large shrew with a long snout. It feasts on insects and worms, delivering its venom down a deep groove in one of its teeth.

The giant anteater has an appetite that's—yup, you guessed it—gigantic. It can stick its tongue out two feet (0.6 meters) and guzzle 35,000 ants and termites a day, all without chewing! It flicks its tongue up to 160 times a minute, so it can down its meal before the insects sting.

Don't Get Me Antsy!

Giant anteaters don't have teeth. But that doesn't mean they're toothless when it's time to defend themselves. When it senses danger, the anteater can stand on its hind legs and attack with its long claws. It will even battle big cats such as jaguars and pumas!

Down on the Farm

Cows, goats, and sheep—boring! **Domestic** animals just stand around chewing their cud and nibbling grass until it's time to be milked, sheared, or taken to market, right? Well, think again!

domestic (duh-MES-tik): no longer wild but kept as a food source, as work animals, or as pets

Not a Leg to Stand On!

Myotonic goats have a curious habit when they're spooked: They faint! The goat's muscles and joints lock up when it's frightened, causing it to fall over and lie stiff for several seconds. That's why this breed is also known as "wooden leg goats" or "fainting goats."

Sheep can recognize the faces of dozens of other sheep—and still recall them two years later! But get this: They can also identify human faces, and not just the familiar farmer or shepherd. Researchers have trained sheep to recognize the faces of movie stars, politicians, and other celebrities.

Got milk? Want more? Play music! Dairy cows that listen to classical music produce more milk. Try playing your cow something by Moo-zart!

Eat More Chicken!

Cows eat plants—it's what herbivores do. Well, sure, most of the time. But some **bovines** have been known to eat chicken—and we mean live, not fried! Scientists believe the cows break their dining habits to replace missing minerals in their diet. At least we now know why the chicken crossed the road!

bovines (BOH-vines): members of a group of animals including oxen, bison, buffalo, and their relatives

Howlers, Poopers, and Sleepers

With their wrinkled little faces, the capuchin monkeys of Central and South America look like wise old people. And these crafty forest-dwellers are certainly smart! Capuchins can be trained as cuddly companions for people with disabilities. The monkey can help people by using its amazing agility and nimble fingers to open bottles, change TV channels, turn on the microwave, or simply scratch an itch!

They're Not Monkeying Around!

For centuries, bearded capuchins in Brazil have used stone hammers and other tools to crack open nuts!

Another tree-dwelling resident of the tropical Americas is famous for its lion-like roar. Howler monkeys have big throats and vocal chambers shaped like shells. They can be heard howling from three miles (five kilometers) away! The monkey's call—which, okay, sounds like a very loud burp—is a warning to other **primates** to stay away.

primates (PRYE-mates): members of the group of mammals that includes monkeys, apes, and humans

Wombats carry their babies in cozy pouches on their bellies. That's interesting, right? These marsupials have rat-like teeth that never stop growing. That's pretty cool too. Wombat poop is shaped like a cube. Say what? We're not kidding. Wombats are the only animal in the world with poop that doesn't come out in, well, a regular poop-shape!

Anyone Have Air Freshener?

Talk about stinking up the neighborhood. Wombats poop 80 to 100 cubes a night, which they place around their burrows to mark their territory.

25

Giant pandas are among the world's rarest animals. Fewer than 2,000 are believed to live in the wild, all in the remote mountains of China. The pandas are born white. Their famous black-and-white coloring develops later.

Shoot, Not Bamboo Again!

Giant pandas have a pretty boring diet: Bamboo for breakfast, bamboo for lunch, and bamboo for dinner. Oh, and some bamboo snacks in between meals! Pandas spend about 12 hours a day chomping on bamboo shoots, leaves, and stems.

Have trouble getting out of bed in the morning? Sloths know just how you feel. These sluggish slackers sleep up to 20 hours a day! A sloth's life is so slow, algae and moths grow and live in its fur to provide **camouflage**. Hey, friend, what's the hurry?

camouflage (KAM-uh-flahzh): a disguise or natural coloring that allows an animal to blend in with its surroundings

Memory Game

Look at the pictures. What do you remember reading on the pages where each image appeared?

Index

armadillo(s) 6
giant pandas 26
kangaroo(s) 4, 8, 9
Komodo dragon 11
monkey(s) 20, 21, 22
sheep 14, 17
sloths 28
wombat(s) 24, 25

After Reading Questions

1. How many ants and termites does a giant anteater eat each day?
2. What happens to myotonic goats when frightened?
3. How does the pink fairy armadillo protect itself?
4. What is a giant panda's favorite food?
5. Where do female marsupials carry their babies?

Activity

Over the course of one day, count how many types of land animals you see. Count pets, farm animals, forest and field animals, and more. Choose one animal and learn an interesting fact about it.

About the Author

Gary Sprott is a writer in Tampa, Florida. His favorite animals at the zoo are the Indian rhinoceros, the Bornean orangutans, and the Siamang gibbons.

© 2020 Rourke Educational Media

All rights reserved. No part of this book may be reproduced or utilized in any form or by any means, electronic or mechanical including photocopying, recording, or by any information storage and retrieval system without permission in writing from the publisher.

www.rourkeeducationalmedia.com

PHOTO CREDITS: Cover: ©Dudarev Mikhail, ©yavdat, ©EEI_Tony; Pg 10 & 30 ©Anna Kucherova; Pg 13 & 30 ©Christian Musat; Pg 16 & 30 ©PeopleImages; Pg 23 & 30 ©reisegraf; Pg 24 & 30 ©keiichihiki; Pg 6 & 30 ©belizar73; Pg 3, 4, 6, 8, 24 ©yavdat; Pg 4-5 ©Etienne Outram; Pg 6 ©Heiko Kiera; Pg 8-9 ©Freder; Pg 9 ©Susan Flashman; Pg 11 ©Sergey Mikhaylov; Pg 12 ©guillaume ©regrain; Pg 14-15 ©Philippa Michael; Pg 17 ©skodonnell; Pg 18 ©mtreasure; Pg 18 ©driftlessstudio; Pg 20 ©Kirsten Walla; Pg 21 ©MikeLane45; Pg 25 ©Mandy Creighton; Pg 26 ©Hung Chung Chih; Pg 26-27 ©ytwong; Pg 28 ©Daniel Lange; Pg 29 ©kengoru

Edited by: Kim Thompson
Cover and Interior design by: Kathy Walsh

Library of Congress PCN Data

Cows Eat Chicken! And Other Strange Facts / Gary Sprott
(That's Wild!)
ISBN 978-1-73161-728-6 (hardcover)
ISBN 978-1-73161-252-6 (softcover)